When POTENTIAL *Meets* PURPOSE

A Journey of Discovery, Growth and Divine Assignment

By Melissa McDuffie and Kenneth McDuffie

CopyRights

WITH GRATITUDE

We offer our heartfelt thanks to every intercessor, mentor, friend, and family member who believed, prayed, and partnered with us. Your faith and love have been instruments in God's hands, shaping this journey from potential to purpose.

Melissa & Kenneth McDuffie

DEDICATION

This work is tenderly and reverently dedicated to our mothers. Women who were living epistles, read by all, whose very breath carried the fragrance of Heaven.

They showed the world what it looks like when potential bows to purpose, when a life fully yielded becomes a vessel of divine legacy.

First, they served their families as if tending a sacred altar. Then, their neighbors, as if every handshake were a covenant and even strangers, as if they were entertaining angels unaware.

Their footsteps were psalms. Their hands, instruments of grace. Their words, quiet prophecies that shaped generations.

Every day, without pulpit or spotlight, they preached faith, modeled grace, and embodied strength that did not clamor for attention, but could not be ignored. Because of them, we stand. Because of them, we believe. Because of them, we are.

Queens, we crown you with our gratitude. Thank you for being the pattern, the prayer, and the proof. Thank you for living your testimony out loud, even in your silent tears.

Rest now, crowned with glory, in the unending embrace of His presence. Your assignment is complete, but your impact echoes in eternity.

Dedication

INTRODUCTION & REFLECTION

Every journey begins with a divine spark; a moment when potential awakens, and purpose whispers its name.

In these pages, you are invited to recognize the image of God within you, to confront what silences your courage, and to embrace the process by which Heaven matures destiny.

May each chapter be a doorway into alignment with the purpose for which you were sent.

IV

FOREWARD

It has been both a joy and an honor to witness the spiritual growth of Melissa and Kenneth McDuffie. As their spiritual leaders, we've watched them walk faithfully through seasons of discovery, development, and divine assignment. Their obedience to God's voice and their passion for helping others fulfill their calling shine through every page of this book.

When Potential Meets Purpose is a timely reminder that our God-given potential isn't confined to the four walls of the Ecclesia. Melissa and Kenneth remind us that purpose goes far beyond the sanctuary, it's found in how we live, love, serve, and show up in our everyday lives.

This book encourages readers to be free from the opinions and comparisons of others, to walk boldly in their God-given identity, and to embrace the unique purpose God has placed within them. It also nudges those who already know their purpose but have grown complacent to develop and steward what God has placed in their hands.

Every chapter invites reflection and alignment, pushing us to see ourselves the way God sees us. Melissa and Kenneth have written a message that will awaken potential, stir purpose, and remind every reader that when potential meets purpose, destiny unfolds.

With Love and Kingdom Blessings,

Apostles D.C and Tara Terry

When Potential Meets Purpose is a short and simple to read, yet extremely powerful! This book will be a favorite because the message it brings is encouraging no matter what challenges a person is going through.

The first prayer says, "Help me to see myself the way You see me!" The rest of the book confirms that prayer. In addition, a declaration and prayer follow each lesson. Each prayer is on point and allows readers to pray when they are not sure what to pray for.

I would recommend this book to readers who are mature in Christ as a source of truth and encouragement as well as to young Christians who need to believe in what their desires are telling them.

Dr. Vickie Dexter,

This book, When Potential Meets Purpose, is not merely a motivational guide or a collection of inspirational thoughts. It is a prophetic journey. A divine summons. A clarion call to become. With every chapter, you will feel the breath of God awakening what has long been dormant, overlooked, or buried beneath fear and delay. You will be reminded that the potential within you is not wishful thinking—it is Kingdom seed waiting for activation.

The authors write with the wisdom of one who has walked through the valley of obscurity and emerged carrying oil. Each word is saturated with both grace and truth, drawing from the wells of Scripture and the experiences of real lives transformed when God's plan breaks through human limitation. You will not only be inspired, you will be provoked to action.

We live in an hour where heaven is demanding a return on what it has invested. The cry of the Spirit is not just for church attendance but for Kingdom fulfillment. The earth groans for the manifestation of the sons and daughters of God (Romans 8:19). That manifestation begins when potential aligns with purpose. When the gift becomes governed. When the heart says, "Yes, Lord," even when the full path isn't clear.

If you have ever felt hidden, silenced, or unsure of your value—this book will be a healing balm. If you are standing at the crossroads of transition, unsure which way to go; this book will shine light on the path. And if you know you were born for more, but don't know how to access it, this book will give you language, direction, and courage.

You were created in the image of a creative God. That means there is innovation in your hands, solutions in your voice, and impact in your very being. But none of it is accidental. You were formed with intent. Designed with destiny. And now, you are being summoned into fulfillment.

As you turn these pages, do so prayerfully. Read with expectation. Highlight with boldness. And most of all, respond with surrender.

Because when potential meets purpose, heaven and earth collide—and destiny is born.

With Love and expectation,

Apostle Pamela B Wise

FOREWARD

Table of Contents

Table of Content

INTRODUCTION

When Potential meets Purpose

There is a defining moment in your life when your potential collides with your purpose. Potential is the capacity God placed within you. Purpose is why He placed you here.

Have you ever felt like your potential was overlooked? Maybe you have been the dependable one, the background support, the quiet strength in the room, yet rarely seen for who you really are. You have carried dreams that others dismissed. You have gifts you were not quite sure how to use. And over time, perhaps you started to wonder, "Does any of this really matter?"

Let me reassure you, it matters deeply. Your potential is not some vague possibility; it is divine evidence that God planted something powerful inside of you. It does not require a platform or a perfect track record. What it needs is a yes. A willingness to believe that you were made for more, even if you cannot see the full picture yet.

You were born with kingdom potential, not by accident, but by divine design. Before you ever took your first breath, heaven had already written your blueprint for your life (Jeremiah 1:5). Your potential is not measured by what others can see, but by what God has already placed within you.

This book is for every person who knows there is more. More to become. More to give. More to activate. As you journey through each chapter, may you uncover hidden strength, heal from what held you back, and awaken the calling within you. Because when potential meets purpose, destiny is revealed.

When Potential Meets Purpose

2

INTRODUCTION

CHAPTER ONE

UNDERSTANDING POTENTIAL

Potential is the divine deposit of what could be; an invisible assignment coded into your spiritual DNA. It is not something you earn; it is something you carry. Potential is Heaven's whisper of destiny wrapped in the raw material of today. It is not just a possibility; it is a promise in seed form. You do not have to create potential; you were born with it.

Before the world gave you a label, God gave you potential. Before life added limitations, Heaven wrote your name into purpose. When God breathed life into Adam, it was not just breath; it was potential. That same breath lives in you. That same creative power speaks into chaos and brings forth order. You are not just here to exist. You are here to expand.

What is Potential?

Potential is Heaven's investment in earth through you. It is the evidence that God intends more for your life than survival. It is the reason you dream of things bigger than your resume. It is the tug in your heart that says, "There must be more." Potential is what God sees when others see your past. It is the treasure in your earthen vessel. And while man looks at what you have done, God looks at what He placed inside of you that is still waiting to be done.

When Does Potential Show Up?

Potential shows up before you ever realize it. Jeremiah 1:5 says, "Before I formed thee in the belly, I knew thee..." Before birth, God had already assigned value. Potential shows up in obscurity, in frustration, in delay. It appears in the wilderness, not the spotlight. You do not grow into potential; you awaken to it. And the moment you say yes, the moment you surrender, the moment you believe that God is still writing your story; that is when potential begins to move.

Who Has Potential?

Everyone. Potential is not reserved for preachers, prophets, or public figures. It lives in the mother raising Kingdom kids. It rests on the janitor who prays over hallways. It whispers in the heart of the teen who journals poems in secret. Potential is not biased by background, limited by labels, or disqualified by detours. If God gave you breath, He gave you purpose; and inside that purpose is potential.

Where Does Potential Lead?

Potential does not lead to applause; it leads to alignment. It pulls you out of comfort zones and into Kingdom spaces. It may lead you through hard places before it takes you to high places. Joseph's potential led him from a pit to a palace. David's led him from the field to the throne. Ruth's led her from gleaning to legacy. Wherever your potential takes you, it is not about elevation; it is about impact. You were never meant to just carry potential. You were meant to release it.

Scripture Foundation

Before I formed thee in the belly I knew thee; and before thou camest forth out of the womb I sanctified thee... Jeremiah 1:5

Chapter One

Kingdom Insight

Potential is not created by effort; it is discovered by alignment. You were formed with divine design, not to blend in, but to reflect a facet of God that the world has never seen before. Your potential is the spiritual wiring Heaven embedded in your soul. It is not about trying harder; it is about surrendering deeper.

Just as electricity requires connection and flow, potential requires obedience and movement. It is power in seed form. You do not need to be discovered; you need to be developed. And development starts the moment you stop waiting for external validation and start responding to God's internal whisper: "I made you for more."

The enemy is not threatened by people who look powerful. He is threatened by people who move in power. And that power is already in you, wired for impact, marked by Heaven, and waiting for activation.

Kingdom in Action

Teresa was a quiet administrative assistant at her local school. For years, she assumed her job was just paperwork and student records. But when a teacher left suddenly, Teresa stepped up to lead morning devotion. Within weeks, students began to gather not just for attendance, but for truth. Teresa was not trying to be noticed. She was simply walking in unlocked potential. Today, she mentors young women across her city; not because she chased a platform, but because she embraced her yes.

When Potential Meets Purpose

Kingdom Applications

What if the stirring in your heart is not just emotional; it is evidence of divine design? What if the tension you feel in your current season is God pushing you to unwrap the next layer of your potential? Your gifts are not random. Your desires are not accidental. God is trying to show you that you were made for more.

Kingdom Activation

Declaration: I was born with divine potential. I refuse to settle for survival when I was created for impact. Fear will not silence my obedience. Comparison will not blur my identity. I carry the spark of God within me, wired for greatness, destined for glory. Today, I stir every dormant gift. I choose alignment over approval and boldness over delay. I am not waiting for permission, Heaven already said yes. Every hidden seed is awakening.

Chapter 1 Summary: Understand Potential

Potential is the invisible assignment coded into your spiritual DNA. It is not earned, it is embedded. From the moment God formed you, He planted purpose within you, waiting to be unlocked, cultivated, and expressed.

This chapter explores the what of potential (your divine capacity), the when (it develops over time, not all at once), the who (you, as a vessel chosen by God), and the where (every season, situation, and setting of your life).

Potential does not wait for a stage; it shows up in surrendered hearts. The moment you begin to see yourself through God's lens, not through fear, shame, or comparison, you activate what has been inside you all along.

God uses even your past pain and current obscurity to train your hands for purpose.

This is your reminder: you are not random. You are not behind. You are in process and that process is power.

When Potential Meets Purpose

8

Chapter One

PRAYER OF ALIGNMENT

Lord, awaken what You planted in me before time began. Let every buried gift rise to the surface. Break the chains of fear, insecurity, and delay. Reveal the areas where I have underestimated Your deposit. Give me the courage to move, even when I do not feel ready. Silence every lie that told me I was not enough. Stir holy confidence in my heart. Help me to trust what You see in me. Let Your power flow freely through my surrendered yes. Today, I activate the potential You placed in me for Your glory In Jesus Christ Name, Amen

When Potential Meets Purpose

Chapter One

CHAPTER TWO

UNDERSTANDING PURPOSE

Purpose is the divine destination embedded in your design. If potential is the seed, purpose is the fruit. It is not a mystery God is hiding from you, but a direction He is unfolding within you. You were not born to simply exist. You were born to express the mind of God in motion. Everything about you, your personality, your story, your pain, your gifting, has been designed with purpose in mind.

Scripture Foundation

For I know the thoughts that I think toward you, saith the Lord, thoughts of peace, and not of evil, to give you an expected end. Jeremiah 29:11

What is purpose?

Purpose is the original intent of God for your life. It is why you were formed, who you were sent to impact, and the Kingdom agenda tied to your existence. You are not a random accident; you are a divine assignment. Your purpose may express itself in different roles throughout your life, parent, teacher, leader, builder, but the foundation is always rooted in God's vision.

When is purpose revealed?

11

Often not all at once. God reveals purpose progressively, like a scroll unrolling one act at a time. Some seasons are for preparation. Others for activation. Some for rest, and others for warfare. You may not always see the full picture, but you can trust the process. Psalm 37:23 says, 'The steps of a good man are ordered by the Lord.' Every step is significant. Even delays, disappointments, and detours can carry destiny.

Who is called to purpose?

Everyone. There is no such thing as a purposeless person. Whether you feel behind, broken, unqualified, or unsure, God has placed something eternal within you. Your purpose is not about being famous. It is about being faithful. Moses did not feel qualified. Esther was afraid. Jeremiah felt too young. But purpose did not skip them. And it will not skip you.

Where is purpose found?

Not just in pulpits or platforms, but in the hidden places, in raising your children, in serving your community, in stewarding your creativity, in starting the business or mentoring the next generation. Purpose shows up in obedience. It thrives in surrendered spaces.

You may be asking, 'Am I really making a difference?' The answer is yes. Every time you show up with integrity, speak life, create in excellence, or help someone heal, you are walking in purpose. You do not have to chase it. You carry it. And as you align with God, purpose begins to unfold naturally, supernaturally, and intentionally.

When Potential Meets Purpose

Kingdom Insight: Understanding Purpose

"Purpose is not something you chase, it's something you carry."

Purpose is the divine intention behind your design. It is not optional, it is essential. Before your first breath, God authored a plan that only your life can fulfill. Purpose is not a future destination; it is a present mandate. It meets you in your morning routine, your quiet prayers, and your willingness to show up, even when it is hard.

While the world may define purpose through performance and platform, Heaven defines it through obedience and impact. Purpose shows up in the classroom and the boardroom, in the kitchen and the pulpit, in tears and in triumph. Wherever you are planted, purpose is already present.

When you stop measuring your life by titles and start measuring it by testimony, everything changes. You were born to carry Kingdom solutions. You are not just in the world; you were sent to transform it. Purpose is your permission to live fully, love boldly, and lead faithfully. This is not just your calling; it is your commissioning.

Kingdom Activation

Declaration: I was created on purpose, for purpose. I am not an accident; I am an assignment. My purpose was written by God and cannot be erased by man. I walk with clarity, courage, and Kingdom authority. Every day I breathe is another opportunity to fulfill my mission. I refuse to wander aimlessly. I will not allow confusion to cancel my calling. God's plan for me is good, strategic, and unfolding in perfect time. I align with Heaven's design. My purpose is clear, and I will walk in it, fully and faithfully.

Chapter Two

Take 10 minutes today and write down the moments in your life that seemed random but actually led to significant breakthroughs or divine connections. These are clues to how your purpose unfolds in motion.

Choose one area of your life where you feel 'on pause' and ask God to show you how purpose is still active there. Then, take one small step of obedience in that direction.

When Potential Meets Purpose

Chapter 2 Summary: Purpose

Purpose is not a distant destination; it is a present-day assignment. It is not just about what you do, but who you become in Christ.

This chapter dives into the multifaceted nature of purpose: what it is (divine direction fueled by Kingdom identity), when it is revealed (in stages, through process), who carries it (you, uniquely designed by God), and where it manifests (wherever you show up with obedience and faith).

Purpose does not wait for perfect timing. It walks through doors opened by willingness and surrender. When potential meets purpose, your life stops being a series of random moments and becomes a sacred journey.

Every step becomes strategic. Every day becomes a divine assignment. You are not simply here to exist, you are here to impact. This is the season where you stop asking for permission and start; living on purpose.

Chapter Two

PRAYER OF ALIGNMENT

Father, thank You for crafting me with intention. I surrender my timeline, my fears, and my distractions. Clarify the vision You have for my life. Let Your Word be a lamp to my path and a fire in my bones. Reveal the places where I have lost focus. Help me to walk in daily obedience to Your voice. I reject confusion and embrace divine direction. Let my choices reflect my calling. Make me sensitive to Your promptings. Today, I align with Your purpose and choose to live it boldly. In Jesus Christ Name, Amen

CHAPTER THREE

THE POWER OF POTENTIAL

The presence of potential is the promise of purpose; It is not waiting for perfection; It is waiting on your yes.

Sometimes we expect our purpose to arrive like a thunderclap. But more often, it whispers in our obedience. It shows up in the courage to start again, in the grace to rise after disappointment, in the quiet decisions no one sees but God.

There is a force greater than talent, deeper than passion, and stronger than will. It is power, not the world's version of dominance, but a divine energy sourced from God Himself. This power is the unseen force that awakens vision, sustains purpose, and advances the Kingdom through yielded vessels. From the very beginning, God made it clear: we were not created to simply exist, we were created to carry something sacred.

"And God said, Let us make man in our image, after our likeness: and let them have dominion" (Genesis 1:26).

That verse is not just theological, it is prophetic. It is your original

17

story, the blueprint of divine empowerment. To be made in God's image is to be filled with divine potential. To reflect His likeness is to carry His power. To rule in the earth as kings and priest.

You were not made by accident. Your capacity is not optional. Your potential is not a bonus feature. It is Heaven's investment, evidence of God's intentionality in your design. The Lord said in Jeremiah, "Before I formed thee in the belly I knew thee; and before thou camest forth out of the womb I sanctified (to be set aside for God's special purpose) the, and I ordained thee. There is a special ordination that God designed for signs, miracles, and wonders.

In the natural world, the Law of Power, as expressed in Ohm's Law, teaches us something prophetically profound: Power = Voltage × Current. Power is the result of what is inside (voltage) multiplied by what is moving (current). prophetically speaking, this means your God, given potential becomes power when it is activated by movement, obedience, faith, and surrender. You can carry potential, but until it is in motion, it will sit idle. You were never meant to just possess voltage. You were created to release power. How do we know this? Let us look into Genesis chapter 2 verse fifteen, God put Adam in the garden of Eden to dress it and to keep it. The first thing God gave Adam is potential.

According to the Law of Conservation of Energy, power can only be transformed, not lost. That means the power God placed in you cannot die. It may be delayed, buried, resisted, or misdirected, but it is not erased. The enemy can distract you, but he cannot dismantle what Heaven has encoded in your spiritual DNA. God's gifts are without repentance, and your power is still waiting to be activated.

Power is not volume. It is not control. It is not attention. Power is divine ability in motion. It is the Holy Spirit working through your surrender. It is the manifestation of potential when it collides with obedience. Power flows when potential aligns with purpose. The Greek word for power in the New Testament is dunamis, where we get the word "dynamite." It is not passive. It is explosive. It is ability, authority, and activation, all in one.

18

Chapter Three

A Hebrew word for power is rashut, this term refers to power in sense of authority, domain, control, or territory. God told Adam to dress and keep the garden. So not only did God give him dunamis; he gave him rashut to acts as kingdom administer with authority reigning in life.

"Now unto him that is able to do exceedingly abundantly above all that we ask or think, according to the power that worketh in us" (Ephesians 3:20). That power is within you. It is not external. Not borrowed. Not manufactured. It is already deposited, waiting for agreement.

Power is often blocked, not because we are uncalled, but because we are unwilling. It is not the absence of gifting that stops many believers, it is the presence of fear. Like a kink in a hose or a break in a wire, spiritual resistance disrupts the flow of Kingdom power. God's power is available, but alignment is essential. Just as electricity cannot flow through a broken circuit, divine power cannot flow where there is persistent disobedience, spiritual doubt, or mental delay.

Consider Moses at the burning bush (Exodus 3–4). He was chosen, called by name, and encountered the raw power of God face, to, face. Yet when purpose called him forward, fear answered first. "Who am I to go to Pharaoh?" he asked. Then came the excuses: "I am slow of speech." "Send someone else." Though God gave him signs, reassurance, and even Aaron to assist him, Moses delayed because he could not see past his own limitations. His insecurity almost silenced an entire assignment. That is what fear does, it clogs the current of power with hesitation and self doubt.

But God was not asking Moses to be perfect, He was asking him to be obedient. The moment Moses stopped resisting and said yes, divine power began to flow. The Red Sea parted. Signs and wonders followed. But it all hinged on that initial surrender.

Excuses delay momentum. Fear short, circuits faith. And comparison clouds our identity, so we forget who we are and Who sent us. When we agree with fear instead of faith, we block the very power Heaven

19

longs to release through us. Power is not given for performance; it is given for purpose. And that purpose requires movement.

Just like Ohm's Law in the natural ($P = V \times I$), power flows when voltage (God's voice) meets current (our obedience). But resistance (fear, doubt, delay) lowers the output. If you want the power of God to manifest in your life, you must remove the resistance and reconnect to the source.

God is not waiting for your perfection. He is waiting for your yes. When fear is silenced by faith, when excuses are exchanged for obedience, and when identity is aligned with assignment, the power flows freely.

God gave Adam dominion before He gave him a platform. Before he built anything, he was called to administrate something. Your life is your Eden, your home, your relationships, your influence, your voice. That territory is not random. It is divine. Power flows when you work the ground God gave you.

"Before I formed thee in the belly, I knew thee... I ordained thee a prophet unto the nations." (Jeremiah 1:5). You were set apart before time to carry power on purpose. Not just to impress, but to impact.

Why the Enemy Fights Your Potential

Have you ever noticed how resistance rises when you begin to move toward your purpose? That is not a coincidence, it is warfare. The enemy does not wait until you arrive to attack; he starts early because he recognizes the threat your potential poses to darkness. Hell, wages war on what Heaven has affirmed.

From the very beginning, Satan was not just after Adam and Eve's behavior, he was after their image. In Genesis 3, the serpent targeted their identity to serve their authority. Likewise, in Matthew 4, Satan tempted Jesus not because He was weak, but because of the power Hell knew He would walk in. Temptation is often a sign that potential is waking up.

If your warfare has been intense, it may be because your potential is

20

too dangerous to go unchecked. The enemy tries to shut down what God has already stirred up. But here is the good news, what God ordained, Hell cannot cancel. When you rise in identity, you silence the lies. When you walk in alignment, you frustrate the plan of the enemy. And when you refuse to bow to fear, your potential begins to prophesy.

Heaven Invests in What You Carry

God does not invest without expecting a return. Your potential is Heaven's deposit. Your power is Heaven's expectation. That is why grace keeps pulling you. That is why prophetic words still echo. That is why you cannot shake the stirring inside. You are carrying something worth warfare. Lisen, power is not passive. It demands stewardship.

"And the yoke shall be destroyed because of the anointing." (Isaiah 10:27). The anointing is what destroys what tried to hold you back. It is not for performance; it is for purpose. When you steward your gift with obedience, the power on your life becomes a divine weapon.

Voltage is your capacity, your gifts, your God, given potential. Current is your obedience, movement, decisions of faith. Power is what manifests when the above align. This is not hype. This is Kingdom order. When you move, power is released. When you agree, Heaven backs you. When you obey, God's presence flows through you. You are both the vessel and the voltage. You are not waiting for power; you are carrying it.

Scripture Foundation

Now unto him that is able to do exceedingly abundantly above all that we ask or think, according to the power that worketh in us. Ephesians 3:10

Kingdom Insight:

The Moment Power Is Released

21

There is a moment, quiet, yet charged with divine voltage when everything aligns. Heaven speaks. Destiny stirs. And suddenly, what once felt dormant begins to surge with holy energy. This is not the time to shrink. This is the hour to stand fully alive, fully charged, fully surrendered.

This is the equation of divine release:

Power equals Potential multiplied by Movement.

God has already placed the voltage of His Spirit within you. The gifts, the wisdom, the anointing, these are not future dreams; they are current realities waiting to be activated. But potential alone is not enough. Just as electricity requires a current to flow, your spiritual power requires movement, obedience, faith, surrender, action.

Every time you chose healing over hiding, growth over fear, forgiveness over offense, you were increasing the current. You were plugging into divine momentum. Heaven was storing your yes like fuel, building spiritual voltage behind the scenes. And now, the switch has been flipped. What has been waiting in the invisible realm is ready to manifest in the visible.

This is more than a shift. It is a surge.

Power does not show up in fanfare. It arrives through alignment. It flows through surrender. It moves through the unseen yes, the hidden prayer, the silent resilience, the persistent obedience. And in that sacred collision of what is in you and what Heaven designed for you, power is released.

This is not about performance; it is about presence. Not about hype, but alignment. You are no longer waiting to become powerful; you are already wired for it. The power of God is not a feeling; it is a force working through yielded vessels.

You become the mother who prophesies while cooking dinner. The pastor who ignites fire in the quiet one. The entrepreneur who builds systems that restore dignity. You stop asking, "Am I enough?" because power is not about your confidence, it is about your connection. And

22

Chapter Three

when you are connected, you cannot be denied.

So walk in it. Speak from it. Build with it. You are not behind schedule. You are not too late. This is your hour. This is your surge.

Kingdom in Action

Consider this testimony. Angela had always loved to sing. From the time she was a child, worship stirred something deep in her. But fear kept her silent. Insecurity wrapped around her gift. Until one Sunday, the worship leader called out. And the pastor looked at Angela and said: "I believe this is your moment." She stepped forward trembling. But when she opened her mouth, glory filled the room. Chains broke. Tears flowed. She did not just sing; she stepped into her power. That yes launched a worship ministry. Obedience activated what had always been within her.

Your power is real. But power flows only when connected. Let go of excuses. Remove the resistance of fear. Say yes to Heaven's yes. You were not created to live idle; you were made for movement. Today is the day you plug in.

Kingdom Applications: When Power Begins to Flow

There is a moment, quiet, but unmistakably divine, when the dormant voltage inside of you finally connects with the current of movement. That moment is now. This is not just inspiration; this is ignition. You are not simply carrying potential; you are becoming power in motion.

For too long, you have stood at the edge of your assignment, sensing the weight of what God placed within, yet hesitating to move. But the equation is simple: $P = V \times I$. In other words, your power is the result of your potential multiplied by your intentional movement. Without motion, voltage remains unused. But the moment you step, speak, or surrender, Heaven flows through you.

23

This is the divine collision where hesitation breaks, and clarity emerges. It does not arrive with applause, but with awareness. You begin to see that every scar holds strategy, every delay had design, and every detour was really divine redirection. What once seemed random now feels orchestrated. You realize you are no longer waiting for purpose; you are walking in it.

Power shows up in your posture. It is in the decision to keep going when no one claps, to show up full even when you feel empty, to speak even when your voice shakes. Every "yes" you whispered in hidden places was building spiritual voltage. Every moment you chose faith over fear was Heaven's way of charging your soul.

You are not second guessing anymore. You are not silencing yourself to fit into rooms that cannot handle your power. You are no longer asking for permission to be what God already ordained. You are aligned, activated, and advancing.

And now, your life becomes a live wire.

Remember, you are the mother igniting prophetic destiny in her children. You are the teacher writing identity into young hearts. You are the quiet mentor with thunder in your prayers. You are the Kingdom builder who creates systems to carry oil.

You are no longer surviving; you are conducting Kingdom power. So rise, Move, and Flow. Let every scar preach. Let every room you enter feel the shift. Let the voltage of your surrender spark awakening in those around you. Because this is not just the end of a chapter, it is the beginning of your surge.

You are no longer just carrying potential; you are a vessel of voltage. You are Power in Motion.

The power of God within you is real, but it can be blocked. Not by lack of gifting, but by fear that silences obedience, by doubt that distorts identity, by comparison that clouds vision, and by delay that disguises itself as preparation. You were never meant to carry potential that stays buried under excuses, insecurities, or shame.

24

Chapter Three

Too many walk around charged but not connected, gifted but inactivated, because power requires agreement. You must say yes to God's yes. Until you surrender the lies, the power cannot fully flow.

You were created with divine potential, not just to exist, but to impact. It is time to stop waiting for permission. Heaven already said "yes." Let go of the lie that you are not enough. Release every excuse, every fear, every delay.

Today is the day you rise in bold obedience. See yourself through the eyes of God, called, chosen, and capable. He is not asking for perfection.

He is asking for your surrender.

Stand in faith. Shake off the dust of fear. Align with power and motion.

Kingdom Activation

Declaration: I am becoming what Heaven already saw, I am not a mistake. I carry God's breath, God's purpose, and God's power. My potential will not be wasted, it will be awakened, developed, and released in Jesus' name. I am not powerless. I carry the dunamis of God. I will not shrink, delay, or hide. I walk in divine voltage. I am not waiting to be empowered; I am already equipped. My potential will not die buried. It will be awakened, stewarded, and released for God's glory. I am power in motion. I am a Kingdom conduit. I will walk in purpose boldly. Because what God placed in me, cannot be destroyed.

Chapter 3 Summary: The Power of Potential

Your potential is not a distant dream, it is a divine deposit already placed within you. In this chapter, you discovered that potential is not something you earn, it is something you carry. It is the God-given capacity to fulfill a Kingdom assignment that no one else can complete the way you can. But potential alone is not enough; it must be recognized, stirred, and submitted.

You learned that comparison, fear, and self-doubt often veil the true power of what is inside you. Yet God, in His grace, uses truth, healing, and faith to reveal and unlock it. Like a seed, your potential is packed with purpose, but it must be planted in surrender and watered with obedience.

Whether you feel qualified or not, what you carry is sacred. The power of your potential is not about being perfect, it is about being positioned. Positioned to grow. Positioned to obey. Positioned to impact. This chapter calls you to stop minimizing your gift, to stop waiting for the right moment, and to start walking in the truth that your potential is powerful, purposeful, and needed now.

PRAYER OF ALIGNMENT

Father, thank You for forming me with power and purpose before I ever knew myself. You placed potential in me to show your greatness in me, not for my name, but for Your name's sake. I repent for doubting what You deposited. Forgive me for the resistance, the delay, and the fear. Awaken every dormant gift. Stir the voltage within. Let boldness replace hesitation. Let alignment override excuses. Make me sensitive to every opportunity to move with You. Help me steward what You have placed inside of me, faithfully and fearlessly. Let the power You breathed into me flow freely. In Jesus Christ Name, Amen

When Potential Meets Purpose

Chapter Three

CHAPTER FOUR

PERSONAL POTENTIAL

What comes naturally to you might be a supernatural lifeline to someone else; own it, use it, be it.

Before you ever picked up a title, job, or role, God gave you an identity. That identity, infused with divine design, holds the blueprint for your personal potential. You are not random. You are not a mistake. Your personality, passions, struggles, and story are all part of the raw material God uses to shape your life.

Many of us spend years searching externally for what God placed internally. But discovering your personal potential is not about finding yourself; it is about learning who God already says you are.

Your personal potential is not hidden in some distant future, it is already living within you, waiting to be embraced. Maybe you have overlooked it because it feels too ordinary. Maybe you have brushed it off because it does not look like anyone else's gift. But the truth is, what comes naturally to you might be a supernatural lifeline for someone else.

Think about the things you love to do; the way you encourage others, the way you bring peace into a room, the way you organize, create, nurture, or teach. Those are not just quirks or hobbies. They are clues. They are glimpses into how God wired you to impact the world.

29

Personal potential is not always loud. It does not always announce itself with titles, status, or applause. Sometimes, it looks like a teenager left out of the lineup. When the prophet Samuel came to anoint the next king of Israel, Jesse called all his sons, except David. Why? Because even David's own father did not see him as qualified. He was "just a shepherd boy," tucked away in the fields, playing the harp and tending sheep. Overlooked. Undervalued. Uninvited. And yet, heaven saw him.

This is what personal potential looks like through the eyes of God: not disqualified by who ignores you but chosen by who created you. Man looks on the outward appearance, but the Lord looks at the heart (1 Samuel 16:7). David's potential was not in his résumé. It was in his heart, his posture, and his willingness to be faithful in the field before ever holding a crown.

Maybe, like David, you have been hidden. Maybe you have been told you were too much, or not enough. Maybe your wounds made you question your worth. But here is the truth: God's anointing is not intimidated by people's opinions. What He placed inside of you is not a mistake, and it does not need validation from those who cannot see your value.

The same sling David used to kill Goliath. It was not a new weapon; it was already in his hand. Your potential might look ordinary, but in God's hands, it becomes a giant, slaying tool.

So yes, start where you are. Use what you have. Be who you are. Because the version of you that you have been hiding, the one shaped by tears, trained in silence, and tested in obscurity, might be the very answer someone else is praying for.

You are not rejected. You are reserved.

You are not late. You are being refined.

You are not forgotten. You are God's strategy in motion.

30

Identity Is the Foundation

Personal potential does not begin with action; it begins with identity. Before you can ever walk in purpose, you must first know who you are in Christ. If your identity is unstable, your purpose will always feel unreachable. You cannot walk confidently in your assignment while questioning your design. Identity is the foundation upon which all Kingdom movement is built.

You were not mass produced. God does not make duplicates. You are an original design, fearfully and wonderfully made, uniquely wired emotionally, spiritually, and intellectually to reflect His glory in a way no one else can. Heaven handcrafted you with distinction and destiny in mind.

That is why comparison is so dangerous. It is not just distracting, it is destructive. Comparison whispers lies that undermine your confidence and distort your assignment. It causes you to abandon your own lane while chasing someone else's. But God did not call you to copy, He called you to carry. You carry something sacred. And until you embrace your divine identity, you will continue to underestimate your divine potential.

The Power of Self, Awareness and Surrender

Unlocking your potential does not begin with action, it begins with awareness. But awareness without surrender is incomplete. Moses shows us what happens when divine identity meets yielded obedience.

Moses was raised in Pharaoh's palace, trained in royalty, fluent in the language of the oppressor, yet deep inside, he sensed a different assignment. One day, his self, awareness stirred: he was not an Egyptian. He was Hebrew. He was born to be a deliverer. But when that awareness was not yet surrendered, it led to premature action. Moses killed an Egyptian and fled to the wilderness, not because the call was wrong, but because his awareness was not yet refined by surrender (Exodus 2).

31

In the desert, Moses became a shepherd. And there, away from the noise of Egypt and the pressure of performance, God began to stir the deeper layers of his potential. The burning bush was not just a call; it was a confrontation. A moment where God said, "You know who you are. Now trust Me with it."

Moses tried to argue. "I can't speak." "I'm not qualified." "Send someone else." But God was not asking for Moses' perfection. He was asking for his surrender. And the moment Moses said yes, even with trembling lips and hesitant faith, the oil began to flow. That yes split seas. That yes delivered a nation. That yes turned a fugitive into a friend of God.

Moses did not become powerful because of position. He became powerful because he surrendered what he knew in exchange for what God said.

And so must we.

Your self-awareness, your insight into your own strengths, weaknesses, and spiritual DNA, is a gift. But without surrender, it can turn into comparison or paralysis. You will see your calling but fear your capacity. You will recognize the gift but resist the assignment.

Surrender is the difference between sitting on potential and releasing power.

You already carry what you need. But it must be stirred. And the stirring happens when you stop striving and start surrendering. That is when Heaven breathes on what is inside of you. That is when God turns raw talent into Kingdom oil.

So lay it down.

Let God use your stutter like He did with Moses. Let Him breathe on the very part of you that once felt like a flaw. Because potential is not activated by striving, t is ignited by surrender.

When Potential Meets Purpose

Cultivating Personal Potential

Potential does not grow by accident. It must be cultivated with intention, faith, and surrender. Like a seed, your potential is powerful but only when placed in the right environment. Left unattended, it remains hidden beneath the surface. But when you partner with God, your seed becomes a harvest.

Obedience is the first atmosphere. It aligns your life with Heaven's rhythm. Every yes to God tills the soil of your spirit. Obedience activates motion, and motion activates momentum. It does not always feel glamorous, but it is always fruitful.

Healing is the next ingredient. You cannot grow around wounds. You must grow through them. When you allow God to heal the broken places, He does not just patch them, He transforms them. He turns your scars into strength and your history into healing for others.

And then comes community. God never intended for you to cultivate potential in isolation. True community waters your roots, not just your fruit. It speaks life when you are weary. It calls forth greatness when you have forgotten it exists. The right people would not let you settle when Heaven says soar.

Finally, discipline brings consistency. Not as a punishment, but as a posture. Discipline in prayer, fasting, worship, and study becomes the structure that sustains your potential. It is not about perfection; it is about alignment. Your habits create the space for your harvest.

You are not behind. You are becoming. Every moment of obedience, every healed wound, every disciplined step is pushing your seed to the surface. Keep growing. Keep moving. Because the soil may be silent, but the seed is working.

Scripture Foundation

For God hath not given us the spirit of fear; but of power, and of love, and of a sound mind. 2 Timothy 1:7

Chapter Four

Kingdom Insight

What if the part of you have always dismissed, your love for encouraging others, your eye for design, your way with words, was not a side note, but a sacred seed? What if the personality traits you once tried to tone down were the very expressions God intended to use to stir revival, healing, and hope?

Too often, we are conditioned to believe that potential must look like someone else's success. We hide our voice. We suppress our creativity. We minimize our uniqueness to fit a mold Heaven never asked us to wear. But God does not create duplicates. You were divinely crafted, with intentional wiring, emotional sensitivity, and spiritual depth that reflect a dimension of Him the world desperately needs.

Your personal potential is not a mistake. It is a mirror of God's imagination. And when you stop apologizing for how you are built and start aligning with the Designer, everything shifts. Your presence becomes impactful. Your story gains authority. Your journey, with all its twists and turns, becomes someone else's breakthrough map.

You do not need permission to show up whole. Your authenticity carries weight. Your truth unlocks doors. Your gifting, no matter how quiet, quirky, or unconventional is a weapon in the hands of a loving God.

This is the season to stop measuring your worth against someone else's calling. It is time to come out of hiding. Time to pick up your full identity and wear it boldly. You were not made to blend in. You were born to become.

Kingdom in Action

Consider this testimony. Janelle always dreamed of launching a nonprofit for women in recovery, but fear kept her stuck. "What if no one shows up?" she wondered. For five years, she postponed the launch. Finally, after a prayerful fast, she booked a room, prepared a lesson, and showed up with trembling hands. Only two women came, but one gave

When Potential Meets Purpose

her life to Christ. That was all Janelle needed. That night, fear lost its hold. Today, her nonprofit serves over one hundred women monthly. Her obedience overcame what fear tried to bury.

Speak life over yourself. Call out what God sees, not what fear says. Embrace your differences. Your uniqueness is a gift, not a flaw. Ask God for insight. Say, "Lord, show me how You have wired me for purpose."

Kingdom Applications

There is a part of you, maybe a habit, a hobby, or a hidden joy; that you have brushed off as not spiritual enough. But what if that very part of you was designed by God to bring healing, hope, or help to someone else? Imagine what could happen if you stopped minimizing your voice, your creativity, or your kindness. Imagine what God could do with your love for organizing, or your passion for encouraging others. Imagine if your rejection was not the end of your story, but the beginning of someone else's breakthrough.

Personal potential is not about being perfect, it is about being present and intentional with what is already inside you. Your gift was never meant to stay dormant. It was meant to serve, to shine, and to shape lives.

Chapter Four

Declaration: There is purpose in my personality. There is power in my process. I will no longer minimize what God has maximized in me.

Today, I choose to confront fear with faith. I recognize that fear is a liar, a thief sent to rob me of divine momentum. I refuse to let the enemy replay failure or magnify insecurity. My voice matters. My calling is real. I may feel afraid, but I will not live beneath my promise. I choose obedience, even in trembling. I choose to move forward, even without clarity. I trust that every step I take is ordered by God.

Chapter 4 Summary: Personal Potential

Personal potential is the internal compass of gifts, passions, and divine wiring placed within you. Before you ever picked up a title, job, or role, God gave you an identity. That identity, infused with divine design, holds the blueprint for your personal potential. You are not random. Your personality, passions, struggles, and story are all part of the raw material God uses to shape your life.

Many people search externally for what God placed internally. Discovering personal potential is not about finding yourself. It is about learning who God already says you are. Your potential may feel ordinary, but what comes naturally to you might be a supernatural lifeline for someone else. The world does not need an imitation. It needs you healed, growing, and fully authentic. Your potential is not based on public validation. It is anchored in divine design. Start where you are, use what you have, and be who God created you to be.

Chapter Four

PRAYER OF ALIGNMENT

Lord, I thank You for giving me power over fear. Your Word declares that I have a sound mind. Today, I silence every lie that says I am not enough. Break the spirit of fear off my life completely. Let courage rise in every place fear tried to reside. Remind me of who I am and to whom I belong. Surround me with strength and clarity. Let my faith move mountains fear built. Help me say yes even when I feel unsure. I will not fear what man shall do unto me. In Jesus Christ Name, Amen

When Potential Meets Purpose

CHAPTER FIVE

PROFESSIONAL POTENTIAL

Your desk is an altar and your work is worship; when you show up in faith, even obscurity becomes holy ground.

Your job is not just a paycheck. Your career is not just a climb. Your professional life is one of the most powerful platforms God can use to advance the Kingdom if you let Him. God never designed work to be separate from purpose. In fact, from the very beginning, He placed Adam in the garden to work it and take care of it. That assignment was not a curse; it was an expression of stewardship.

Today, many believers separate the sacred from the secular. But in the Kingdom, there is no divide. Whether you are teaching in a classroom, serving meals, coding software, or leading a boardroom, your work matters to God. It is not about position; it is about purpose.

You may find yourself in a workplace that does not reflect your worth. The title may not match your talent. The tasks may feel tedious. And your heart may be quietly wondering, "Is this it?" But do not be discouraged. Your professional potential is not limited to a job description; it is rooted in your calling.

39

God often uses our careers as classrooms. That challenging coworker might be sharpening your patience. That tight deadline might be building your resilience. That season of obscurity might be preparing you for influence that would not break you when it comes. Do not rush past the lesson in search of the spotlight. What feels like a delay may actually be divine development.

Purpose does not wait for a promotion. You can show up in excellence today, even in places where you feel unseen. Every email you write, every shift you work, every project you touch, it can all carry Kingdom impact when done with intention and grace. And maybe, just maybe, the role you are in is the very ground God is using to plant something greater. Joseph interpreted dreams in prison before he ever stepped into the palace. Ruth gleaned in the fields long before Boaz noticed her. Your current position might not be the finish line, but it is holy ground.

It is important that we ask God, "What are You doing in me through this job?" Because when your work becomes your worship, your desk becomes your altar, and your daily grind becomes a stage for His glory.

What if your workplace is your mission field? What if your desk is your pulpit? What if your professionalism is your witness? You do not have to be in full, time ministry to serve God. You simply need to be fully available where He has placed you. Your professional potential is not about being the best in the world, it is about being the most faithful with what God has entrusted to you.

Excellence is not perfection; it is doing the best you can with what you have been given. And it speaks volumes. The spirit of excellence sets believers apart because it reflects the character of the God we serve. When you show up on time, work with integrity, respect others, and solve problems, you are not just doing a job. You are displaying the Kingdom. We read from Proverbs 18:16, "A man's gift maketh room for him, and bringeth him before great men." Your gift makes room for you, but excellence builds the platform God can use.

Your career may change, but your calling is constant. It is not what you do, it is why you do it. A calling is the deep, God, given pull toward how you serve the world. And your professional potential is often where

When Potential Meets Purpose

calling, and competence collide. Sometimes, God will call you to plant deeply in a profession. Other times, He may call you to pivot. Either way, it is obedience that activates destiny, not titles.

Scripture Foundation

And whatsoever ye do, do it heartily, as to the Lord, and not unto men…
Colossians 3:23

Kingdom Insight

There is no divide between sacred and secular when God is involved. Your career, your craft, your business, it is random. Heaven never designed you to compartmentalize your calling. Your professional life is not a detour from ministry. It is ministry.

You may feel like your nine to five is ordinary. You might see your trade, your office, your business as just a means to survive. But God sees it as fertile ground for Kingdom impact. The workplace becomes a pulpit when excellence becomes your offering. The conference room becomes holy ground when you carry compassion into conflict. Your skillset is not just functional, it is anointed.

God often reveals destiny through diligence. When you show up consistently with character and creativity, Heaven moves through what your hands produce. You do not need a collar to carry calling. You do not need a title to carry weight. You just need alignment. And when your professionalism is submitted to the purpose of God, favor follows.

You were not placed where you are by accident. Whether you are leading a team or serving behind the scenes, you are positioned for transformation. Your workplace is a mission field. Your integrity is evangelism. Your diligence is discipleship. And your influence, no matter how visible or quiet, is undeniable.

Let your work preach. Let your excellence speak volumes. And let your profession become the platform through which God gets all the glory.

Chapter Five

Kingdom in Action

Listen to this powerful testimony. Marcus worked as a janitor at a local high school. While some overlooked him, the students did not. He knew all their names. He showed up early, prayed over the halls, and mentored young boys quietly during lunch breaks. One student told him, "You are the reason I did not drop out." Marcus never stood on a stage, but his hallway became a pulpit. He maximized his position, and God used him to change lives. That is professional potential in motion.

Pray for purpose at work. Invite God into every decision, meeting, and task. Serve with intentionality. Look for ways to reflect Christ through your actions. Identify the assignment that is around you.

Kingdom Applications

You may be in a job right now that feels like a detour, a place that does not quite match the dreams God whispered to your heart. Maybe you are working long hours in a role that seems unnoticed, or your creativity feels caged in a system that does not see your value. It is tempting to believe that this space is wasted, but friend, God wastes nothing.

That difficult workplace? It may be the very ground where your patience is being cultivated. The monotonous tasks? They may be sharpening your diligence and humility. That supervisor who tests every fiber of your grace? God may be using them to build in you a strength that cannot be shaken.

You do not have to wait for a new title or promotion to walk in purpose. You can start today, right where you are, by inviting God into every detail. Because when your work becomes worship, even your profession becomes a Kingdom Mandates.

When Potential Meets Purpose

Declaration: My work is worship. My job is an assignment. I bring excellence, integrity, and faith into every space I enter. God is using me to influence others through my profession.

Today, I choose to honor God in my work. I will show up with integrity, joy, and purpose. I recognize that my workplace is not just about tasks, it is about testimony. Every moment I give my best, Heaven takes notice. I will no longer shrink in spaces where I was sent to shine. Whether I lead or serve, I will do all as unto the Lord. My hands carry purpose. My voice carries weight. My work matters to the Kingdom, and I will maximize every opportunity to reflect God's Kingdom.

Chapter 5 Summary: Professional Potential

Professional potential is more than a job title or career success; it is the sacred expression of God's purpose in the marketplace. This chapter explores how your work is not separate from your calling but an extension of it. God has equipped you with talents, insight, and influence that are meant to bring transformation into the spaces you serve, lead, or build.

Whether you are behind the scenes or in the spotlight, your professional space is holy ground. The chapter emphasizes the importance of character over charisma, integrity over image, and purpose over promotion. It reminds you that God uses your skill set, creativity, leadership, and problem-solving ability to impact lives and shape culture.

Even if your current position feels small, God is watching how you steward it. Faithfulness in your assignment unlocks favor for the next. You are encouraged not to compartmentalize your faith and work but to invite the Holy Spirit into every decision, meeting, and opportunity. Professional potential is about being excellent, not just successful, being impactful, not just impressive.

God is not looking for professionals who simply climb ladders; He is raising up Kingdom professionals who build bridges. When you realize that your career is a calling, you stop striving and start serving with divine clarity. Your profession becomes your platform for purpose.

When Potential Meets Purpose

PRAYER OF ALIGNMENT

Father, thank You for trusting me with influence through my work. Help me to walk in integrity and spiritual excellence. Let my coworkers see Christ through my attitude and actions. Anoint my assignments with Your wisdom and favor. Remind me daily that my work is a witness. Use me to shift the culture around me for Your glory. Open doors that align with my calling. Let Your Spirit guide my decisions and conversations. Help me to labor with joy. In the Mighty Name of Jesus Christ, Amen.

Chapter Five

When Potential Meets Purpose

CHAPTER SIX

DEVELOPMENTAL POTENTIAL

You are not stuck; you are stretching. Quiet growth in hidden seasons produces deep, lasting fruit

Growth is not a suggestion in the Kingdom; it is an expectation. From the moment you gave your life to Christ, a divine process began inside of you. Not one of instant arrival, but of ongoing transformation. The goal of salvation is not just to get to Heaven; it is to become more like Jesus on the way there.

Second Peter 3:18 says, "But grow in the grace and knowledge of our Lord and Savior Jesus Christ…" That word "grow" implies movement, expansion, stretching. Spiritual maturity does not happen by accident; it requires surrender, intention, and consistency.

If we are honest, most of us love the idea of growth, but we resist the process of it. Because growth, by nature, is uncomfortable. It asks you to leave what is familiar. It pulls you out of your safety zone. It exposes your weak spots so God can strengthen them.

To develop, you must remain open, teachable, and willing to be corrected and willing to be changed. Developmental potential is not just about acquiring new skills, it is about receiving divine instruction with humility

Chapter Six

and applying it with faith. God develops what you are willing to surrender.

But here is the truth: God is not looking for perfection; He is looking for progress. He does not grade you on how fast you grow, but that you are still growing. Every step forward, no matter how small, matters deeply to Him.

Spiritual and personal development is not just a "nice to have," it is God's command. The moment you were saved, you were called into a lifelong process of transformation. The goal of your walk with God is not just to go to heaven, but to become more like Christ on the way there.

God is not looking for perfection. He is looking for progress. Your developmental potential is the invitation to become everything He envisioned when He formed you. Maybe you are in a season where growth feels more like survival. You are still showing up, still praying, still serving but deep inside, you wonder why progress feels so slow. You may look around and think, "I should be further along by now." But spiritual growth does not always look like victory laps. Sometimes, it looks like quiet endurance.

You are not stuck. You are stretching. Growth in the Kingdom is rarely glamorous. It is forged in the hard, hidden places where no one is clapping and nothing feels certain. But those are the moments where depth is born. God is not just interested in what you do for Him; He is interested in who you are becoming with Him.

Transformation takes place in the furnace of consistency. It happens when no one is watching, when you choose prayer instead of pride, obedience instead of offense, patience instead of quitting. In those sacred moments of surrender, you are being shaped.

But here is the key: you must remain teachable.

A teachable spirit is the soil where Kingdom fruit grows. Without humility, there is no harvest. Without correction, there is no elevation. And without surrender, there is no transformation. Growth is not just about doing better; it is about becoming more like Him.

48

"The way of a fool is right in his own eyes: but he that hearkeneth unto counsel is wise." Proverbs 12:15

The Holy Spirit is your Counselor. He is not only your Comforter, but your teacher. He reveals blind spots, illuminates scripture, and prunes your character to prepare you for purpose. When you yield, He transforms.

Yes, growth can be painful. Trees stretch. Muscles tear. Faith is tested. But the tension is necessary. The pressure is divine. Do not run from the discomfort, it is shaping your next dimension.

Just ask Joseph.

He was given a dream in his youth, a vivid vision of leadership, honor, and destiny. But instead of instant elevation, Joseph faced betrayal by his brothers, slavery in Egypt, and false accusation that led to years of imprisonment. Imagine the silence of those prison walls. No applause. No confirmation. No visible fruit.

But growth does not always happen in public.

In that hidden place, Joseph learned to manage resources, steward favor, and trust God in obscurity. Each trial was not a denial of the dream, but a divine classroom for his character. His faithfulness in the unseen prepared him to manage a nation in the spotlight. What looked like stagnation was divine cultivation.

Like Joseph, you may still wrestle with old fears or prayers that seem unanswered. But do not misread the silence. God often does His deepest work underground. Roots grow before fruit appear.

Your consistency in prayer, resilience in trial, and obedience in the unknown are all stretching your spiritual capacity. Every tear, every test, every hidden moment, it is preparing you not just to arrive at destiny, but to sustain it when you get there.

So keep going. Like Joseph, your faithfulness in this season is setting the stage for your next one.

And here is the good news; spiritual development is not about sprinting; it is about surrender. God is not measuring you against someone else's

49

timeline. He is walking beside you, patiently shaping your heart. Every quiet yes, every step back toward Him, every time you choose to stay rooted instead of running, it matters.

You do not have to feel on fire to be growing. Sometimes, the greatest growth happens in the middle of your most uncertain days. Keep going. Keep trusting. The fruit is coming.

Every stage of growth has a stretch. Trees do not grow without pressure from within. Muscles do not build without tension. Likewise, your spiritual and emotional growth will require pain, pruning, and perseverance. Do not mislabel discomfort as punishment, it is often the fertilizer for your potential. What feels like pressure may be God preparing you for greater capacity.

God has not left you to grow alone. The Holy Spirit is your teacher, guide, and strength. He convicts, comforts, and empowers you to break unpleasant habits and build new ones rooted in Christ. When you yield to the Holy Spirit, He will shine light on hidden patterns, invite you into healing, and shape your character to sustain your calling.

We often want quick transformation, the "suddenly" moments. But most growth happens daily, not dramatically. It is showing up in prayer even when you do not feel like it. It is choosing forgiveness again when bitterness creeps in. It is keeping your word when no one is watching. Growth is cumulative. And God is faithful to finish what He starts.

Scripture Foundation

Being confident of this very thing, that he which hath begun a good work in you will perform it until the day of Jesus Christ.   Philippians 1:6

Kingdom Insight

Growth does not always feel glorious. Sometimes it looks like hidden tears, silent progress, and daily decisions no one celebrates but Heaven.

When Potential Meets Purpose

Development is the space between your yes and your release. It is where God shapes what others will one day see.

There are seasons where you feel unseen, undervalued, or unqualified, but it is in those very places that God is cultivating resilience, refining character, and building capacity. You are not delayed. You are in development. And everything God is doing in you is necessary for what He is preparing through you.

Before David held a crown, he held a harp. Before Esther walked into the palace, she walked through preparation. Before Jesus performed miracles, He matured in favor and stature. Your process is not punishment, it is preservation. You are not just becoming skilled. You are becoming anchored.

There is a version of you God sees on the other side of this. More rooted. More ready. More radiant with glory. The pressure is not breaking you; it is building you. And while others might overlook your progress, Heaven is measuring your obedience.

Do not rush the refining. Trust the timing. Embrace the tension. Because your next requires a version of you that will not break under weight. You do not just need anointing, you need depth. And this is where it is formed.

James 1:3, 4 teach all believers this truth, "Knowing this, that the trying of your faith worketh patience.4 But let patience have her perfect work, that ye may be perfect and entire, wanting nothing."

Kingdom in Action

Monica was abandoned by her husband after 15 years of marriage. The betrayal shattered her confidence, and for a year she barely spoke. But in the quiet, God began to rebuild her. She started to journal her pain. One entry became a blog. That blog became a support group. Today, Monica helps women heal from emotional trauma and find their identity in Christ. Her pain gave birth to a ministry she never imagined. What nearly destroyed her became the very place God displayed His glory.

Identify a growth area. Is it patience? Faith? Leadership? Healing?

51

Chapter Six

Commit to a growth plan, scripture study, mentorship, accountability, prayer. Celebrate progress. God rejoices over every win.

Kingdom Applications

Maybe you have hit a wall in your spiritual growth. You still love God, still serve, still show up. However, deep down, you feel stagnant as if you have been circling the same lessons, the same frustrations, the same prayers that have not yet been answered. It can feel like you are stuck. But what if you are not stuck, what if you are simply in a stretch?

Growth does not always come with fireworks. Sometimes, it comes in quiet, persistent obedience. You may not feel like you are making progress, but God is always working, especially in the hidden places. What you call delay; heaven may call development.

Or maybe you are frustrated with how long it is taking to see change in your character. You still lose your patience, still wrestle with fear, still feel like you "should be further by now." But friend, God is not in a hurry. He is not measuring you against someone else's timeline. He is walking with you step by step, and every small decision toward growth matters more than you know.

Even if your spiritual life feels like it is on pause, remember this: transformation does not happen in an instant. It happens through daily choices. Through showing up in prayer even when you feel nothing. Through choosing kindness when anger feels easier. Through repenting when you fall and getting up with grace again. Progress in the Kingdom is not about how fast you grow. It is about the impact that you make.

Kingdom Activation

Declaration: I am not stuck. I am stretched. Every day, I am growing into the image of Christ. My process is producing purpose. My potential is maturing in the hands of God.

Today, I choose to believe that my pain has purpose. I refuse to let

When Potential Meets Purpose

suffering silence my surrender. Though I may not have all the answers, I trust the One who holds them. I will not hide my wounds or be ashamed of my scars. Healing is possible and restoration is near. God is turning every broken place into a testimony. He is redeeming every disappointment and breathing on every dry place. I say yes to healing, yes to wholeness, and yes to the glory that is to come.

Chapter Six

Chapter 6 Summary: Developmental Potential

Development is not about perfection. It is about progression. Spiritual growth is expected in the Kingdom, and it requires surrender, consistency, and a teachable heart. True growth is forged in quiet obedience, not public applause. God is not concerned with how fast you grow but that you continue to grow.

Even in silence and uncertainty, He is shaping you. A teachable spirit and a heart surrendered to the Holy Spirit create the soil for transformation. Growth may come with pressure, pain, or pruning, but it is never wasted. What you feel stretching you is preparing you for your next. You are not stuck; you are being shaped for greater capacity.

When Potential Meets Purpose

PRAYER OF ALIGNMENT

Father, thank You for being near in times of trouble. Even when I do not understand, I trust Your hand. Take every piece of my pain and make it holy. Heal the places I have hidden in shame and silence. Let my scars speak of Your goodness and power. Make beauty rise from every place I have wept. Let the oil of joy flood every grieving place. Teach me how to minister through what tried to break me. I surrender every wound to Your refining fire.

Like trees pushing through the soil or muscles being built through resistance, your spiritual maturity will be formed through pressure. Do not run from it. Trust that God is preparing you for something greater.

You are not in a holding pattern; you are in holy development. And what God is building in you will be the foundation for what He does through you. In Jesus Christ Mighty Name, Amen.

Chapter Six

When Potential Meets Purpose

CHAPTER SEVEN

SITUATIONAL POTENTIAL

Where you are is not a detour; it is divine preparation. Purpose grows in the places you least expect.

Have you ever found yourself asking, "Why am I in this place?" Maybe the scenery does not match the vision God gave you. Maybe you are working a job that feels beneath your gifts, stuck in a town you did not plan to stay in, or walking through a season that seems too quiet, too slow, or too hard. But what if this very place is part of your purpose? Sometimes, we think purpose will only be manifested once we get to the right place, when the job changes, when the opportunity comes, when the audience shows up. God is a Master of using this place, yes, even this confusing, frustrating, hidden place. He can develop something in you that could not be formed anywhere else.

David was anointed king but went right back to tending sheep. Ruth showed up to glean leftovers in a field before she ever met Boaz. Jesus lived in obscurity for 30 years before preaching His first sermon. Your situation may not look significant, but if God has placed you in it, it is not a mistake. He is working in the background, developing your character, your sensitivity, and your strength.

Instead of asking, "How soon can I leave this?" try asking, "What is God trying to teach me here?" Your situation may be stretching you, but it is also preparing you. Sometimes the promotion is not an elevation in title, but in trust, wisdom, and spiritual maturity.

Purpose does not wait for perfect conditions. It grows in surrendered hearts, wherever they are planted.

David did not start on the battlefield; he started in the pasture. Long before Goliath, there were sheep. And it was in that ordinary, overlooked environment that God trained his hands for war. Likewise, your now is preparing you for your next. That job you cannot stand, the small group you lead, the caregiving, the parenting, the recovery, God is using it to develop grit, trust, and obedience.

Situations are temporary, but their impact can be eternal. Joseph was thrown into a pit, sold into slavery, and imprisoned unjustly. Yet, every setting was used by God to elevate him to a place of influence. This is the power in Kingdom perspective, seeing every challenge as preparation, not punishment.

Sometimes, God will allow frustration in a familiar place to launch you into a new one. He uses discomfort to drive decisions. He allows closed doors to redirect your focus. He uses delays to develop your discernment. Ask not just why you are in a place, ask what God wants to do through you while you are there.

Scripture Foundation

And we know that all things work together for good to them that love God, to them who are the called according to his purpose.   Romans 8:28

Kingdom Insight

Not every season feels spiritual. Sometimes you find yourself in a space that looks nothing like your prophecy. A job you did not plan. A city you did not choose. A relationship that feels heavy. And yet, even there, especially there, God is working.

Chapter Seven

Situational potential is often hidden in places you wish you could escape. But God does some of His greatest work in uncomfortable circumstances. He used a prison to elevate Joseph. A desert to prepare Moses. A lion's den to promote Daniel. And He can use your situation too.

You do not have to understand it to be transformed by it. The trial you are facing may not be your fault, but it still carries your future. God wastes nothing, not the delay, not the diagnosis, not the disappointment. Every environment you have walked through has been engineered for your growth.

What looks like restriction is often revelation.

That workplace may be your training ground. That detour may hold your destiny. That struggle may be the soil where your voice takes root. God never misses a detail, and He is not improvising with your life.

The key is not to escape your current situation, but to embrace it with Kingdom perspective. You are not buried. You are being planted. And what grows from this will carry fruit that impacts generations to come.

Kingdom in Action

After losing a job he loved, Terrence took a part-time position at a coffee shop just to make ends meet. He hated it, until God told him, 'This place is ministry." He started praying over orders, encouraging customers, and mentoring a young coworker battling depression. That coffee shop became a Kingdom outpost. A year later, he was offered a leadership role in a nonprofit company that merged everything he learned from that small place. What looked like a setback became a divine setup.

A

sk God to help you see the purpose of where you are. Look for who you can serve or encourage in your current space. Document what the Holy Spirit reveals to you.

Kingdom Applications

59

Have you ever looked around and wondered, "Why am I here?" Maybe it is not where you expected to be. Maybe your current season feels hidden, heavy, or even humiliating. It can be disorienting when your surroundings do not reflect the dreams God put in your heart. But before you dismiss your location, take a closer look. Because purpose often hides in plain sight. Your current setting might be more sacred than it seems.

Perhaps you are in a role that feels beneath your capacity. You have vision, but you are doing tasks that feel menial. You have dreams, but life looks ordinary. The truth is some of God's greatest promotions are disguised as quiet seasons. Ask David. Before he faced Goliath, he was shepherding sheep, alone, unseen, and overlooked. Yet it was in that quiet pasture that his hands were trained for the battle that changed history.

Or maybe you are in a difficult environment, at work, in your family, or even inside your own thoughts. It is easy to pray for God to move you out. But sometimes, He is trying to move through you first. Your character is being forged. Your discernment is being sharpened. Your dependence on God is being deepened in ways success could never accomplish.

And if you feel invisible, remember so did Joseph in the prison, Ruth in the fields, and Esther in the palace before her moment came. Their stories remind us: God sees what others do not. He is not just preparing the next season; He is preparing you for it.

So instead of asking how soon you can leave the place you are in, try asking what God is trying to teach you. Because where you are, could be the very ground where your next level is being planted.

Kingdom Activation

Declaration: Where I am is not where I will always be. But while I am here, I will grow, serve, and prepare. God is using this season to sharpen my purpose and build my strength.

I may not understand why I am here, but I choose to trust the God who placed me. This place has purpose. I will no longer curse my location; I will cultivate it. Every season carries an assignment, and I will not miss mine.

60

Chapter Seven

Whether I am visible or hidden, God sees me. I will be faithful where I stand until God moves me forward. My steps are ordered. My situation is not a mistake. I declare that this place has purpose, and I will not miss what You are doing. I activate situational potential with my obedience, and I trust God to elevate me.

Chapter 7 Summary: Situational Potential

Situational potential reveals that where you are is not random. It is part of God's preparation. Sometimes, the place you did not choose is the place God uses most. Your current situation may feel limiting, hidden, or frustrating, but God is developing something in you right where you are. Situations do not have to look spiritual to be sacred. The detour, the delay, the unfamiliar environment; all of it is being used by God to build your faith, character, and readiness. Joseph was promoted through prison. David was anointed but still sent back to sheep. Ruth gleaned in a field before meeting Boaz.

Situational potential teaches you to look for purpose in your present. It teaches you to serve faithfully, even when the stage feels small. When you surrender your current setting to God, He reveals how even this season is aligned with your purpose. You are not stuck; you are being shaped.

PRAYER OF ALIGNMENT

Father, thank You for placing me where You see fit. Even when I feel overlooked, I know You have a plan. Help me to see the opportunity in this place. Let me serve with excellence and joy right where I am. Refine my character through every situation. Use my obedience as a testimony to others. Remind me that hidden seasons still have value. Shift my perspective when frustration arises. Make this place my altar, not my prison. In the Mighty Name of Jesus Christ, Amen

When Potential Meets Purpose

64

Chapter Seven

CHAPTER EIGHT

UNLOCKING POTENTIAL

Unlocking your potential does not require noise; it requires movement. Be bold. Be lit. Turn the key.

You can be gifted and still stuck. You can be called and still feel caged. You can have dreams, ideas, and God given potential, but unless it is unlocked, it stays dormant.

Unlocking potential is the process of releasing what God placed inside of you, removing the barriers of fear, shame, and doubt, and stepping into a life of freedom and fruitfulness. It is the shift from knowing you are called, to walking in it boldly.

Have you ever felt like there is something inside you, powerful, purposeful, pregnant with impact, but you do not quite know how to release it? It is like you are standing at the edge of something significant, but the "how" still feels foggy. That stirring you feel is not just ambition, it is a holy signal that your potential is ready to be unlocked.

Unlocking potential begins with permission. Not from others, from you. You must give yourself permission to step forward, to try, to grow, to fail forward.

Many people remain trapped not because they lack gifts, but because they are waiting for someone else to validate what God already confirmed within. Your gifts are not waiting on a perfect opportunity; they are waiting on your bold obedience.

It may feel intimidating to start. Maybe you are afraid of what people will think. Maybe you are unsure how it all fits together. But let me encourage you, every unlocked door starts with a step. That first conversation, that journaling session, that quiet yes in prayer, it matters. The key to unlocking your potential is movement. Start moving, and God will meet you there.

Just look at Gideon.

When God called him a "mighty man of valor" (Judges 6:12), Gideon did not feel mighty, he felt small. He was hiding in a winepress, threshing wheat in fear, convinced that he was the least in his family and that his tribe was the weakest in Israel. He questioned the angel. He hesitated. He needed signs. But despite all of that, he moved.

That first, trembling act of obedience, tearing down his father's altar to Baal in the dark of night, set off a divine chain reaction. Heaven did not wait for Gideon to feel confident. Heaven responded to his step of faith.

And from that moment on, Gideon's potential began to unfold. God trimmed his army down from thirty-two thousand to just three hundred, reminding him, and us, that obedience is the key to unlocking what God already placed inside. Gideon's potential to lead, to fight, to free a nation was not newly given. It had been there all along, waiting for one surrendered "yes."

You do not need to have it all figured out. What you need is to trust the One who placed the potential inside you in the first place. As you walk in faith, the steps will become clearer, the vision sharper, and the opportunities that once seemed sealed shut will begin to open, not because you forced them, but because you were ready.

A woman who experienced childhood trauma believed she was unworthy to lead. After going through counseling and spiritual healing, she began mentoring girls facing similar challenges. Her healing became the key to unlocking her leadership potential.

Chapter Eight

Many believers live beneath their capacity because of lies they have believed from the enemy within, outside voices and family traditions. 'I am not enough.' 'I have missed my chance.' 'My past disqualifies me.' These lies become spiritual locks that must be broken with truth. Satan knows he cannot destroy your calling, so he tries to convince you it is unreachable.

You do not unlock potential through effort alone. You do it through truth, truth about who God is, about who you are, and about your circumstances. You are not alone in this process. The Holy Spirit reveals truth, heals wounds, and gives you boldness to walk out what God has declared.

Often, our potential is locked behind unhealed pain. God does not just want to use your gifts; He wants to heal your heart. You may need to forgive, release guilt, or let go of fear. Healing is not weakness. It is the gateway to power.

Scripture Foundation

If ye be willing and obedient, ye shall eat the good of the land.

Isaiah 1:9

Kingdom Insight

Potential does not disappear, it gets buried. Beneath trauma. Beneath fear. Beneath the lies you have believed and the labels you have accepted. But just because it has hidden does not mean it is gone. It is waiting on truth, on healing, on surrender.

Unlocking potential is not about striving harder. It is about surrendering deeper. It is choosing to lay down the mask, confront the wound, and silence the voice that told you, you are not enough. It is about letting God excavate the you that has been trapped under performance, comparison, and pain.

God does not unlock you with shame. He does it with love. One revelation at a time. One layer at a time. And as He gently removes what

Chapter Eight

does not belong, what has always been inside begins to rise. Confidence emerges. Clarity returns. And calling becomes visible.

The most powerful version of you is not the one who performs. It is the one who is free. Free from needing applause. Free from proving your worth. Free to create. Free to lead. Free to walk boldly in what Heaven has already approved.

This is the moment when your identity becomes louder than your insecurity. When your potential is no longer locked behind your past but released into your future. And it all begins with a yes.

Kingdom in Action

Clarice had always dreamed of leading, but childhood trauma made her question her worth. At a women's retreat, she felt God say, "The time is now." She was terrified. But she submitted her story to the pastor and asked to lead a group. That first group transformed lives and hers. Clarice now leads a growing mentorship network for young women who feel silenced. Her healing unlocked her leadership. And her obedience unlocked a Kingdom assignment.

Kingdom Applications

Have you ever felt like something inside you was waiting to break free? Like you are carrying something powerful, an idea, a gift, a calling, but it stays buried under layers of fear, shame, or self, doubt? You are not alone. Many people live with incredible potential but never experience the fullness of it, because unlocking that potential takes more than awareness. It takes healing. It takes courage.

Maybe you have believed the lie that you are not ready. Maybe you have replayed the failure, the rejection, or the trauma so many times that it has become a wall between you and your purpose. But here is the truth: God is not intimidated by your past. He is ready to use it as a key.

That lie that whispers, you are not enough, replace it with His Word that says, "You are fearfully and wonderfully made." That voice that says, "You have missed your moment." Silence it with the truth. "God makes everything beautiful in its time." It is not too late.

Freedom does not always come with fanfare. Sometimes, it comes quietly, in a moment of prayer, in a step of obedience, in a willingness to believe again. Sometimes, unlocking your potential starts with forgiving yourself for not starting sooner.

You do not have to have all the answers. You just need to say yes. Yes, to truth. Yes, to healing. Yes, to movement.

God is not waiting for a perfect version of you. He is waiting for a surrendered one. Once you unlock what is inside, you will not just walk in purpose, you will help unlock others too.

Kingdom Activation

Declaration: I will not hide. I will not shrink. I will not settle. God has unlocked something powerful in me, and I am walking forward with clarity, courage, and conviction.

Today, I choose to unlock what is within me. I will no longer wait for the perfect moment to move. My obedience is my key. I refuse to let fear keep the door shut. I trust that what God has placed inside of me is enough. I will no longer bury ideas, delay purpose, or silence my voice. This is my time. Heaven has already said yes. I declare that I am walking in divine release. The vault of potential is open. The door of destiny is swinging wide.

Write and replace lies with truth from Scripture. Ask the Holy Spirit to fill you with confidence and clarity. Take the first step.

69

Chapter 8 Summary: Unlocking Potential

Potential must be unlocked through truth, healing, and bold action. Many people remain stuck not because they lack gifts but because fear, shame, or doubt has trapped them. Unlocking begins when you give yourself permission to move forward and trust the God who placed potential inside you.

The Holy Spirit plays a crucial role in revealing truth and healing wounds that have kept you bound. Movement, even in small steps, activates momentum. Your past does not disqualify you; it may be the very path God uses to prepare you for impact. You are not powerless. You are positioned. And when you say yes to truth and surrender, God unlocks everything within you that has been buried.

Chapter Eight

PRAYER OF ALIGNMENT

Lord, I thank You for the power You placed inside of me. I surrender my hesitation and activate my yes. Let every gift, idea, and purpose awaken now. Break every chain that has locked me out of my calling. Let divine courage rise in every fearful place. I trust that You are unlocking every delayed assignment. Surround me with people who will stir my faith. Let my life reflect the boldness of obedience. Today I move forward with power and clarity. If I be willing, I will eat the good of the land. In Jesus Christ Mighty Name, Amen

When Potential Meets Purpose

Chapter Eight

CHAPTER NINE

MAXIMIZING POTENTIAL

You would not maximize what you would not move on; steward your gifts like worship and watch purpose multiply.

There is a pivotal moment in your journey where recognizing your potential is not enough anymore. God never intended for you to stop at discovery, He desires for you to fully develop, refine, and release what He has placed within you. Unlocking your gifts is powerful but maximizing them is the point. That is where purpose becomes impact. That is where faithfulness becomes fruitfulness.

To maximize your potential means to live with full intention. It is choosing to rise above complacency, silence the voice of doubt, and push past the fear of failure. It means saying no to comfort and yes to calling. It means deciding that "almost" is no longer good enough. You are not here to live halfway. You were created to overflow.

You have seen glimpses of your potential; the leadership, the creativity, the compassion, and the brilliance. But now the question is, what are you doing with it? Are you growing it? Stretching it? Or are you sitting on it, quietly hoping someone will give you permission to act?

73

Let me say this clearly; you do not need another sign. You do not need perfect conditions. You need movement. Delayed obedience is often disguised as disobedience. When we wait too long to act, we miss windows God designed for breakthrough.

It is time to sharpen your edge. Enroll in that course. Seek out that mentor. Reorganize your schedule around your purpose. Write the vision, pray over it, and start executing with bold faith. This is not about striving; it is about stewarding. It is not about being perfect, it is about being present. And every bit of effort you invest is not just shaping your future; it is impacting every life connected to your destiny.

To whom much is given, much will be required. Luke 12:48

In Matthew 25, Jesus tells the Parable of the Talents. The master gave his servants various sums, some more, some less, but he expected them all to multiply what they were given. Two of the servants honored that. One did not. Out of fear, he buried his gift, and was called lazy, not cautious. Let that sink in. God expects increase, not excuses. He honors multiplication but corrects stagnation.

Many of us live in the land of "almost." Almost healed. Almost started. Almost believed. But almost is not the same as answered. God is calling you into fullness, not fragments. The real enemy of your purpose is not failure, it is comfort. Comfort convinces you that survival is enough. But you were made for more. And more always requires motion.

To maximize your potential, you must embrace discipline and diligence. Consistency matters more than applause. Focus matters more than visibility. Discipline matters more than gifting. Yes, the anointing opens doors, but discipline keeps you in the room. The Holy Spirit will help you, but growth still requires your participation.

Just look at Daniel.

He was not elevated in Babylon because of charm or connections; he was elevated because of consistency. From the moment he resolved not to defile himself with the king's food (Daniel 1:8), Daniel lived a life of intentional obedience. He showed up daily in prayer, even when it was illegal. He studied. He interpreted dreams. He governed with integrity. He did not bend to the pressure of culture, and because of that, his diligence distinguished him.

Daniel's anointing made him wise. But it was his discipline that made him trustworthy.

When jealous officials sought to destroy him, they could not find fault in his conduct or character. Why? Because he maximized what God gave him. His life was a masterclass in spiritual and professional stewardship. He was not just gifted, he was faithful.

And here is the Kingdom principle: God promotes those who steward well.

If Daniel had only relied on his prophetic gift but neglected his spiritual habits, his influence would have been short, lived. But his lifestyle, built on the pillars of prayer, excellence, and perseverance, created a legacy that outlived empires.

You may have the gift. But do you have the grit to guard it? You may have the dream. But are you willing to discipline your days so that your destiny does not collapse under neglect?

Daniel did not maximize his potential overnight. It was his daily decision to stay aligned with God that elevated him decade after decade, even in exile, even under pressure, even in the lion's den.

You do not need to be the loudest or the fastest. You need to be the most faithful. Stay consistent. Stay sharp. Stay willing.

Scripture Foundation

For unto whomsoever much is given, of him shall be much be required. Luke 12:48

When Potential Meets Purpose

Kingdom Insight

Potential is the raw material. Purpose is the blueprint. But it is stewardship that builds the structure. Many are gifted. Many are called. But only those who commit to developing what they have been given walk in fullness.

Maximizing potential is not about chasing perfection, it is about choosing intentionality. It is about showing up when no one is watching, refining your gift when applause is absent, and building when the platform seems far away. It is the daily grind of obedience that turns oil into overflow.

God never gives you potential to sit dormant. What He places in you is meant to multiply. But it does not grow by accident, it grows by decision. By discipline. By alignment. Your "maybe one day" becomes "now" when you stop waiting and start moving.

This is the season to stretch. To invest in the version of yourself that carries vision. To become the vessel that has not only filled but is fruitful. God does not bless laziness. He blesses movement. He blesses faith in motion.

You do not need another confirmation; you need a commitment. Because what God placed in you is too powerful to remain buried. You are not here to play it safe. You are here to steward, multiply, and advance. This is your season to maximize what is already in you.

Kingdom in Action

Terrell led worship for years, but he only sang what others told him. One day, God gave him a melody during prayer. He was nervous but shared it. That song became a healing anthem for his church. Another woman, Jasmine, had survived abuse and trauma. For years, she stayed silent. But after mentoring teens at her church, she wrote a devotional for young women. It now reaches girls in group homes across the region. They did not just have potential, they maximized it.

Take time this week to audit your calendar. Are your daily choices aligned with your divine calling? Where are you investing your time, and is it bearing fruit? Make a list of what needs to shift. Then commit to one small step; take a class, start journaling, seek accountability, or launch the idea that has been on your heart. Track the fruit of your obedience. Purpose grows through motion.

Kingdom Applications

There comes a time when recognizing your potential is not enough, you have to run with it. Maybe you have already identified your gifts. You have seen glimpses of what God placed inside you. But now comes the real question: Are you developing it? Or have you settled for "good enough"?

You might feel a tug right now, a restlessness that says, "I was made for more." That is not ambition speaking; that's divine urgency. It is the Holy Spirit nudging you out of complacency and into commitment.

Sometimes, we hide behind the comfort of calling without stepping into the cost of cultivation. It is easier to talk about potential than to do the challenging work of maximizing it. But God is not just looking for gifted people, He is looking for faithful ones. Faithful in the mundane. Faithful in obscurity. Faithful in excellence when no one claps.

If you have been coasting on raw talent, it is time to sharpen your edge. If you have been saying "one day," make today your starting line. Take the class. Refine the message. Build the habit. Write the vision. Set the schedule. Because potential without discipline stays potential. But potential with action? That becomes fruit.

And if you are wondering whether your effort matters, remember this: God sees. He honors every intentional step you take. Your growth is not in vain. Your work is not wasted. The seeds you are planting through diligence, focus, and obedience will one day become a harvest that not only blesses you but everyone connected to you.

When Potential Meets Purpose

Kingdom Activation

Declaration: I will not bury what God has given me. I will grow it, guard it, and use it. I will not waste potential; I will maximize it for His glory.

Today, I choose to multiply what God has given me. I will no longer bury my gifts in fear or insecurity. I declare that I am a good steward of time, talent, and treasure. Every resource Heaven placed in my hands is sacred. I commit to using my voice, my creativity, and my story to glorify God. No more delays. No more excuses. I activate the fullness of who I am in Christ, and I move with intention and power.

Chapter 9 Summary: Maximizing Potential

Maximizing potential means refusing to settle for partial progress. It requires discipline, consistency, and bold commitment. God did not design you to stop at discovery; He expects you to develop and release what He placed inside you.

Talent alone is not enough. You must sharpen your gifts, steward your time, and stay focused even when recognition is absent. Like the servants in the Parable of the Talents, God expects multiplication, not maintenance. You are accountable for what you carry. Your diligence is worship, your progress is purpose, and your daily decisions shape legacy. Now is the time to move from potential to impact.

Chapter Nine

PRAYER OF ALIGNMENT

Father, thank You for trusting me with purpose. I acknowledge the potential You placed within me. Help me to steward my time and gifts with diligence. Break the spirit of fear that tries to paralyze my progress. Let creativity and boldness flow freely in my life. Surround me with divine accountability and grace. Reveal the areas where I have been hiding out of comfort. Ignite every dormant idea You have entrusted to me. I will not bury what You called me to build. In Jesus Christ Name, Amen

When Potential Meets Purpose

CHAPTER TEN

WHEN POTENTIAL MEETS PURPOSE

You have not missed it; you are right on time. Purpose is not a destination; it is a lifestyle. Live it aloud.

This is the moment everything aligns. The divine collision where the potential you carry meets the purpose for which you were created. It is not loud or flashy, it is holy. It is the moment you begin to walk not in uncertainty, but in clarity; not in hesitation, but in bold, surrendered steps.

When potential meets purpose, everything begins to make sense. The confusion fades. The questions about your ability to impact quietly cease. Every scar now tells a story. Every detour has value. You stop chasing validation and start living on assignment. You are not trying to prove who you are; you finally believe it.

This is not about a platform or applause. It is not about perfection. It is about presence. Purpose shows up in consistent surrender, in daily obedience, in whispered prayers and faithful yeses. You realize that you no longer need to become, you already are.

All the identity you reclaimed, all the healing you allowed, all the growth you committed to, it has brought you to this sacred juncture. And what once felt random now feels divinely orchestrated. The trials, the tension,

80

the hidden years, they were not wasted. They were preparation for what God intended for you.

You have moved from wondering if you are called to walking like you are. From sitting on the sidelines to stepping into your own lane. You stop imitating and start embodying. Your voice carries weight. Your presence carries purpose. And you stop apologizing for showing up full.

This moment is not a finish line. It is the beginning. A new chapter of intentional, purpose, driven living. You show up not just as someone with potential but as someone walking fully in purpose. Every step becomes a testimony. Every day becomes a divine assignment.

You become the mother raising world changers. The teacher planting identity in young hearts. The entrepreneur creating opportunities for Kingdom impact. The quiet leader shaping culture without needing to be seen. You are purpose in motion. So, live it. Live it fully. Live it boldly. Live it faithfully.

You have not missed it. You did not disqualify yourself. You are right on time. This is your season. This is your lane. This is the moment when potential meets purpose, and you say yes.

Just ask Moses.

He was called from birth, protected as a baby, raised in Pharaoh's palace, yet he ran, hid, and spent forty years in obscurity tending sheep in Midian. By the time God called his name from the burning bush, Moses felt disqualified by his past, insecure in his speech, and disconnected from the destiny he once sensed. But God never forgot his potential.

In that moment, purpose found him again. Not in the palace, but in the wilderness. Not with a crowd, but in holy solitude. And what seemed like delay was actually divine development. The same rod that once led sheep would part seas. The voice he thought was too weak would speak to Pharaoh. The hands he thought were unqualified would carry the commandments of God.

81

That was the moment when Moses' potential met divine purpose, and he finally said yes.

So do not count yourself out. God specializes in using those who feel behind, unworthy, or uncertain. Your "burning bush" moment may come when you least expect it. And when it does, you will not just walk in purpose, you will release deliverance for others.

Now is your moment. Let your yes ignite generations.

Scripture Foundation

And thine ears shall hear a word behind thee, saying, this is the way, walk ye in it, when ye turn to the right hand, and when ye turn to the left. Isaiah 30:21

Kingdom Insight

There is a moment when everything aligns. The pain, the promise. The gift, the grind. The healing, the hunger. Suddenly, what once felt fragmented makes sense. The pieces form a picture. The wilderness births clarity. And you realize: you are not just carrying potential; you are walking in purpose.

This is the moment where movement replaces hesitation. Where obedience is not a struggle, it is a lifestyle. Where the same hands that once wiped tears now build systems, mentor leaders, birth ministries, shift atmospheres. Your yes has graduated into legacy.

But purpose does not announce itself with trumpets. It shows up in the little things, your consistency, your posture, your response to divine instruction. It lives in the quiet yes, the silent no, the boundaries you protect, and the truth you embody. It is not always loud, but it is always weighty.

When potential meets purpose, the ordinary becomes oil. Your scars

When Potential Meets Purpose

gain strategy. Your story becomes a signpost for others. You are no longer striving for significance; you are moving in Kingdom sync. You have stopped questioning if you are ready. You have decided to trust the One who called you.

This is not the end of your story. It is the beginning of your legacy. You have moved from potential to purpose, not because you figured it all out, but because you chose to show up anyway aligned, with God's calling on your life.

Kingdom in Action

After years of wrestling with fear and rejection, Lisa finally said yes to God's nudge to lead a Bible study in her neighborhood. She had no degree, no credentials, just a burden. Week by week, women came. Tears flowed. Healing happened. What began in her living room became a regional women's movement. Lisa did not wait to be qualified. She simply walked in purpose and God did the rest.

Take a moment to pray. Ask God to clarify your assignment. Write it down. Let it guide your decisions. Eliminate distractions that do not align with your God given assignment.

Chapter Ten

You have journeyed through identity, healing, growth, and boldness. You have wrestled with lies, rediscovered your gifts, and taken inventory of the calling within. And now, you stand at the threshold of alignment. This is more than inspiration; it is commissioning. Because once potential meet's purpose, your life can no longer remain the same.

Maybe you have lived years with dreams stored in journals, ideas whispered in prayer, and gifts you kept on the shelf out of fear. Maybe you have walked through detours that made you question if purpose was still possible. But let me assure you, every detour, delay, and disappointment were shaping your path. Nothing was wasted.

Purpose does not always announce itself with lightning bolts or applause. Sometimes it slips in through quiet conviction and courageous consistency. It looks like the teacher who realizes she is not just instructing; she is imparting legacy. Or the entrepreneur who sees their business as a vessel of healing. It can even be the parent who stops questioning their impact and starts discipling their children with joy. When your gifts, your heart, and your story all point in the same direction, you will know you are not chasing purpose anymore, you are walking in it.

And the best part? You have not missed it. No matter how far you feel you have wandered, purpose has a way of finding you again. It was written into your very being. And now that you have discovered the power of what is inside of you, go make impact for the Kingdom of God.

Declaration: I was made on purpose. I am walking in purpose. My potential is no longer buried, it is active. My life matters, and my destiny is unfolding daily by the power of God.

I choose to walk in purpose, not someday, but every day. I release the need to have it all figured out. I surrender my fears, my doubts, and my delays. I trust that God has ordered my steps and will make divine connections. I will not let comparison silence my movement. I will show up where I am, with what I have, knowing God can multiply it. Purpose is not a place I find; it is a lifelong journey.

Chapter Ten

This is the moment where everything aligns. It is not just a breakthrough; it is a divine intersection where everything you have walked through begins to make sense. The process, the pain, the waiting, it all becomes fuel for purpose. What once felt distant now becomes a divine invitation. You no longer wonder if you are called; you walk as one who knows it. The hesitation fades. The questions quiet. Your voice grows steady. Your vision gains focus.

When potential meets purpose, clarity replaces confusion. You begin to live with intention, speak with boldness, and move with Heaven's rhythm. Your obedience becomes your momentum, and the faithfulness cultivated in hidden places becomes the oil for visible impact. Purpose is not a final destination; it is a lifestyle of consistent surrender and divine alignment.

This chapter reminds us that purpose is not always loud. It shows up in daily obedience, in whispered prayers, in the posture of a yielded heart. It is not about striving to become; it is about accepting that you already are. You realize that the scars you carry now speak with power. Your story becomes a strategy for others. Your life becomes a signpost of what is possible when someone fully surrenders to the will of God.

This is not the end, it is the beginning of intentional, purpose-driven living. You are not late. You are right on time. Every detour was preparation. Every delay was development. And now, you stand as one who is not just full of potential, but walking fully in purpose. You do not wait for permission. You do not shrink in doubt. You are the move of God, and your whole life becomes a bold, unapologetic yes.

When Potential Meets Purpose

PRAYER OF ALIGNMENT

Lord, I thank You for the gift of purpose. Today, I surrender every excuse and delay. Lead me in paths of righteousness for Your name's sake. Give me boldness to walk in what You have called me to. Let my steps be aligned with Heaven's rhythm. Use my life to reveal Your glory. Remove distractions and double mindedness from my path. Let every gift in me come forth and be used for good. Order my steps in Your word, O Lord. In Jesus Christ Mighty Name, Amen.

Chapter Ten

FINAL CHARGE

YOU WERE BORN FOR MORE.

This is not the end of a chapter ; it is the beginning of a movement. The stirring inside of you is not random. It is divine evidence that Heaven has assigned you to manifest potential and walk boldly in purpose.
Every seed of identity that was reclaimed...
Every fear that was confronted...
Every step of growth, surrender, and obedience...

It has brought you to a tipping point ; where your power
must be activated, your voice must be heard, your presence
must be felt, and your purpose must be lived.

No more shrinking. No more delay. No more questioning whether you are enough. You are not behind; you are right on time. You carry weight in the spirit. You are a carrier of glory. You were called to be a Kingdom solution in the earth. The world is not waiting for another copy. It is waiting for your authentic obedience.

So rise.
Build.
Speak.
Serve.
Move.
Become.

Let every page of this book become fuel in your belly and fire in your bones. Let your "yes" echo through every assignment, every room, every generation. May the heavens respond to your obedience and the earth reap the fruit of your surrender.

You are where power meets purpose. You are
the answer someone is praying for.

Now go. Unlock. Activate. Advance. Because destiny is waiting.

88

When Potential Meets Purpose

Romans 10:8–11 (KJV)

But what saith it? The word is nigh thee, even in thy mouth, and in thy heart: that is, the word of faith, which we preach; That if thou shalt confess with thy mouth the Lord Jesus, and shalt believe in thine heart that God hath raised him from the dead, thou shalt be saved.

For with the heart man believeth unto righteousness; and with the mouth confession is made unto salvation. For the scripture saith, Whosoever believeth on him shall not be ashamed.

Come.

This is your divine moment of invitation. Heaven is not far, it is near. The Word is already in your mouth and written upon your heart. This is not a distant call. It is immediate, personal, and holy. God is not asking for perfection; He is drawing you with love.

You are not just being saved from something; you are being called into something, into a Kingdom that cannot be shaken. A Kingdom where identity is restored, voice carries authority, and life becomes a divine assignment. This is not religion; this is relationship. This is redemption.

Let every excuse fall. Let every delay be broken. Let every lie lose its grip. The voice of God is near. The Kingdom is at hand. His Spirit is reaching for you now.

You were never meant to live at the mercy of the world's systems. You were born for dominion. To carry light in dark places. To reveal Jesus in your generation. To walk in righteousness, not religion.

The altar is not a stage, it is your heart. And the confession is not complicated. Believe. Speak. Receive. Rise.

Say yes to the King. Say yes to purpose. Say yes to the divine exchange, where your ashes become beauty, your shame becomes strength, and your voice becomes a trumpet for Heaven's call.

This is more than salvation, it is your sending. You are not just entering the Kingdom. You are becoming an ambassador of it.

So step forward. Speak what God says. Believe what He promised. Walk in what He has prepared. The Kingdom is calling. Say yes.

ABOUT THE AUTHORS

Ambassador Melissa McDuffie answered the call to ministry in 2001 under the leadership of Pastor James A. Owens at Lincolnville Baptist Church. Upon accepting the divine call God placed on her life, she began to faithfully preach and teach the Gospel of Jesus Christ. Melissa lives by Romans 10:9, which declares, "If you confess with your mouth and believe in your heart that Jesus is Lord, you will be saved." She is a visionary leader, mentor, and servant of God with a heart for empowering people to rise beyond limitations. Her work in ministry and the community has transformed lives through identity coaching, spiritual development, and purpose, driven leadership. She brings wisdom, compassion, and insight to everything she does, especially in helping others see what God sees in them.

Ambassador Kenneth McDuffie answered the call to ministry in 2011 under the leadership of Pastor Jerry and Agnes Green at Perfecting the Heart Worship Center. Upon accepting the divine call God placed on his life, he began to faithfully preach and teach the Gospel of Jesus Christ. Kenneth lives by Romans 10:9, which declares, "If you confess with your mouth and believe in your heart that Jesus is Lord, you will be saved." He is a dedicated Kingdom Ambassador, minister, teacher, and motivator. His passion lies in equipping others with biblical truth, prophetic clarity, and practical tools for victorious living. With years of experience in ministry leadership and mentoring, Kenneth is committed to Unlocking divine within every believer.

Their unwavering commitment to God led to elevation and greater responsibility, serving under Pastor Jerry Greene of Perfecting the Heart Worship Center in Chester, South Carolina. There, Melissa and Kenneth served as an Evangelists

When Potential Meets Purpose

and as members of the Board of Directors. It was during this time that they met and later married.

Together, the McDuffies embarked on a deeper season of spiritual training under the leadership of Apostle Raquel D. Broadie, Overseer of the Restoration Apostolic International Network in Charlotte, NC. After much prayer and seeking the Lord, they obeyed God's call to shepherd His people in Chester, South Carolina, where they founded Repairer of the Breach Evangelistic Ministry.

Today, the McDuffies continue to serve faithfully in ministry as Apostles under the spiritual covering of Apostle DC Sr. and Apostle Tara Terry of The Kingdom Learning Center. They are committed to equipping believers, perfecting the saints, and edifying the Body of Christ for Kingdom advancement. They also carry out a prison ministry in Chester County, preaching freedom to those who are physically bound yet called to live free in spirit.

Their ministry operates under the authority of the Holy Spirit, with signs, wonders, and miracles following.

About the Authors

SCRIPTURE FOUNDATIONS BY CHAPTER

Chapter 1: Understanding Potential

"Before I formed thee in the belly I knew thee; and before thou camest forth out of the womb I sanctified thee...," Jeremiah 1:5

Chapter 2: Understanding Purpose

For I know the thoughts that I think toward you, saith the Lord, thoughts of peace, and not of evil, to give you an expected end. Jeremiah 29:11

Chapter 3: The Power of Potential

Jeremiah 1:5 (KJV)

"Before I formed thee in the belly I knew thee; and before thou camest forth out of the womb I sanctified thee, and I ordained thee a prophet unto the nations."

Psalm 139:13–16 (KJV)

"For thou hast possessed my reins: thou hast covered me in my mother's womb. I will praise thee; for I am fearfully and wonderfully made: marvelous are thy works; and that my soul knoweth right well... in thy book all my members were written, which in continuance were fashioned, when as yet there was none of them."

Chapter 4: Personal Potential

2 Timothy 1:7 (KJV)

"For God hath not given us the spirit of fear; but of power, and of love, and of a sound mind."

Chapter 5: Professional Potential

Colossians 3:23 (KJV)

"And whatsoever ye do, do it heartily, as to the Lord, and not unto men."

ScriptureFoundationsbyChapter

Chapter 6: Developmental Potential

Job 23:10 (KJV)

"But he knoweth the way that I take: when he hath tried me, I shall come forth as gold."

Chapter 7: Situational Potential

Romans 8:28 (KJV)

"And we know that all things work together for good to them that love God, to them who are the called according to his purpose."

Chapter 8: Unlocking Potential

Isaiah 1:19 (KJV)

"If ye be willing and obedient, ye shall eat the good of the land."

Chapter 9: Maximizing Potential

Luke 12:48 (KJV)

"For unto whomsoever much is given, of him shall be much required."

Chapter 10: When Potential Meets Purpose

Isaiah 30:21 (KJV)

"And thine ears shall hear a word behind thee, saying, This is the way, walk ye in it..."

When Potential Meets Purpose